COLONIAL AMERICAN
★ ★ ★ CRAFTS ★ ★ ★
The Home

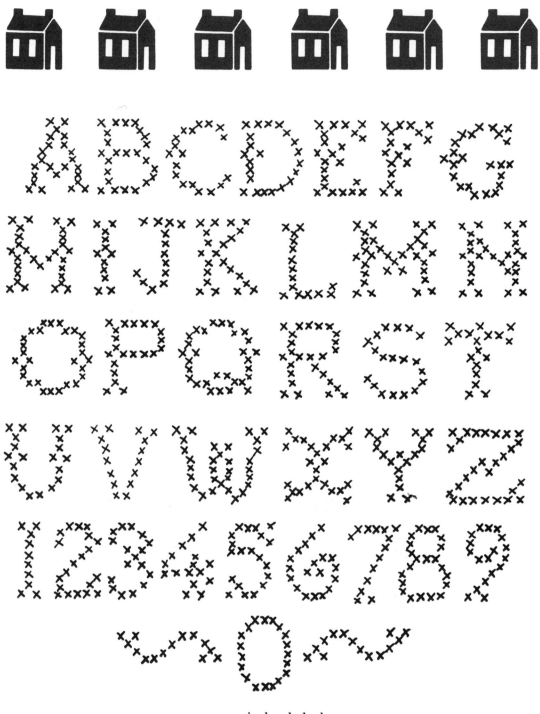

cross-stitch alphabet

COLONIAL AMERICAN
★ ★ ★ ★ CRAFTS ★ ★ ★ ★

The Home

By Judith Hoffman Corwin

FRANKLIN WATTS
New York/London/Toronto/Sydney/1989

For Virginia Dare,
the first child born of settlers
in this brave new land
(August 18, 1587),
and all the others that followed,
especially, my son, Oliver Jamie.

Library of Congress Cataloging-in-Publication Data
Corwin, Judith Hoffman.
    Colonial American crafts : the home / by Judith Hoffman Corwin.
      p. cm.
    Includes index.
    Summary: A collection of thirteen projects and recipes which relate
to the colonial of American home and the way of life there.
    ISBN 0-531-10713-2
    1. Handicraft—United States—Juvenile literature. 2. Cookery,
American—Juvenile literature. 3. United States—Social life and
customs—Colonial period, ca. 1600–1775—Juvenile literature.
[1. Handicraft. 2. Cookery, American. 3. United States—Social
life and customs—Colonial period, ca. 1600–1775—Juvenile
literature.] I. Title.
TT23.C66 1989
745.5—dc20   89-8958 CIP AC

Contents

1700s embroidery design

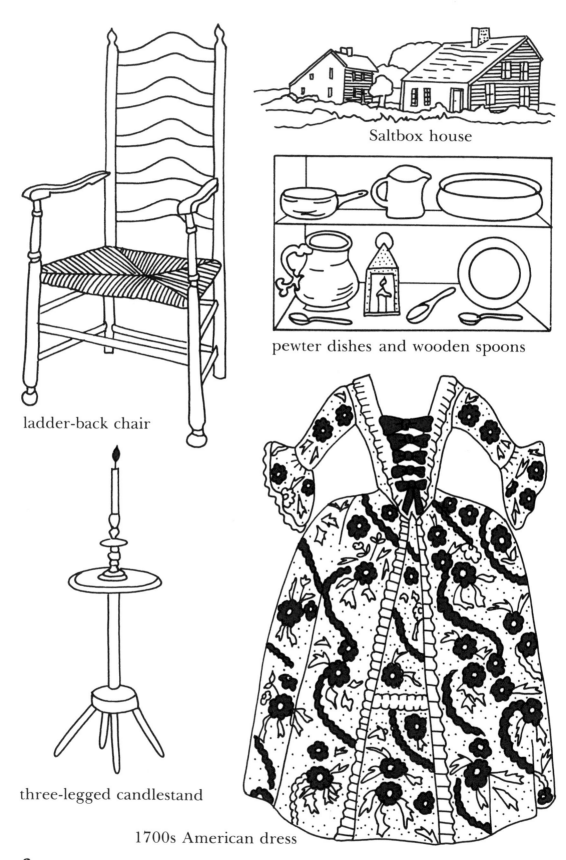

Saltbox house

pewter dishes and wooden spoons

ladder-back chair

three-legged candlestand

1700s American dress

About This Book

This book deals with the colonial period in America, from about 1607 to 1776, just before the signing of the Declaration of Independence. During this time, the colonists were settling into their new environment and were establishing a new life for themselves. We will discover that everyday things—houses, furniture, clothes, tools, food, toys, dishes, candlesticks, and even nails—can all express the character of the time in which the colonists lived.

The first European immigrants to the vast untamed coast of America came to Plymouth, Massachusetts; to New Netherland (which is now New York state); to the Middle Colonies such as New Jersey, Pennsylvania, Maryland, and Delaware; to North and South Carolina; and to Virginia. These first settlers braved the challenge of survival in an unknown land thousands of miles from familiar surroundings, family, and friends. They came for many different reasons, such as the possibility of a brand-new way of life that offered religious freedom, a chance to own their own land, or the promise of a better future.

The colonists came from many countries—England, France, Holland, Germany, and Spain. They brought with them their different customs and skills. There was an exchange of cultures between these settlers and the first Americans—the Indians. The combining of these cultures and the cleverness of using the materials that were found in the "New World" resulted in a new and exciting way of life.

The living conditions were simpler then, and the general knowledge of the first settlers was less extensive than it is today. Daily life was similar to what it would be like for us on a camping trip. Life depended on the weather and on the seasons. Settlers had the bare necessities of life and few possessions.

The colonists found it very hard work to survive in this strange, new land. If they were lucky enough to live through the rough sea voyage, many died during their first years here. They relied on the friendly Indians for help in learning how to grow new foods like corn, cranberries, pumpkins, and squash and where to hunt and fish. The settlers built homes for themselves and their families. At first, some dug caves in the hills or built tipis like the ones the Indians lived in. Other early structures were made from logs with sailcloth stretched over them and raised stockades.

Eventually, the people were able to build and develop towns with wood frame, stone, and brick houses; a mill; a blacksmith's shop; taverns; a schoolhouse; a bakery; a print shop; a lacemakers' shop; a music shop; a general store; a church; a meetinghouse; and even a wigmaker's shop. By the year 1733, there were thirteen colonies. The men and women had to know how to plant and harvest crops, tend to livestock, cook and preserve their own food, make candles, weave cloth, make their own clothes, shear sheep, cure ills, forecast weather, and even embroider and sew patchwork quilts. Children worked hard alongside their parents in order for their family to survive and eventually prosper.

When America was young, almost everything people needed was handmade. The colonists took great pride in the things that they made for everyday use. These everyday items were functional, and many were beautifully crafted. Early American colonists gave us a heritage rich in charming customs and wonderful arts and crafts. We can learn from what they were able to develop and make use of.

Honesty, hard work, a sensible nature, and the ability to work together to solve their problems enabled the colonists to survive in a hostile environment. Try to imagine what life was like in the 1600s and 1700s in this young country. Open, unexplored, bountiful land; natural resources beyond belief; and natural beauty. No car, bus, or airplane noise. All food was grown on your land or nearby or caught in the forest.

There was no fast food, and no radio, television, or home computers. There was no electricity or gas for lighting, warmth, or cooking. Your food was cooked on the open hearth in the middle of the kitchen. Your clothes were made at home by someone in your family, fashioned out of linen or wool made on your farm. You had only a few changes of clothes, and probably only one pair of shoes. Bicycles, skateboards, video games, chocolate bars, and ice cream would not be in your world.

One of the values of history is that it enables us to better understand both the people of other times and ourselves. A peek into the world of eighteenth-century America, when the nation was just beginning, is an exciting look at a trying time, but also a time of opportunity for new beginnings and a chance to be free.

There are three books in the "Colonial American Crafts" series—*The Home*, *The Village*, and *The School*. All three have participation projects that use crafts to provide insights into the lives of colonial people.

spinning wheel

grandfather clock

The Home

During colonial times, families were very large, with lots of relatives living together. There were often six or seven children in one family. A popular proverb of the day was "Children are a poor man's wealth." To the struggling early settlers, every child meant an extra hand with the never-ending work of providing food, shelter, and clothing for the family. Every family member had his or her own chores to do. The men and boys did the hunting, fishing, farming, and caring for the farm animals. Girls also worked in the fields, tended the animals, filled the wood box, spun wool, wove cloth, made the clothes, prepared the food for the family, and cared for the younger children.

As soon as children could do any work at all, they were given a job to do. This set a good example and made everyone responsible for the well-being of the family. This system also made it possible to maintain a household without the many timesaving devices that we have today. There was little time for play. Children were dressed like miniature adults and had to act "grown-up." They were even judged by adult standards. By the age of two, children would be allowed to sit at the table with the rest of the family and eat what the others were eating. Today parents have a variety of books available on how to raise children, but during colonial times the only manuals that dealt with children were extremely strict and had few practical suggestions. Childhood was a very short time—by fourteen, the boys had to go to work; at sixteen, they had a military obligation to deal with. Most girls were married by seventeen or eighteen.

Women did countless domestic chores, worked in the fields, tended the animals. They were supposed to obey their husbands and be content with a subservient position in the society that they did so much to maintain. Women couldn't participate in community life outside of the family, and few colonial women were well educated. These strong, courageous, industrious women had few outlets to express themselves.

Children were born at home. The delivery of the baby by a midwife with the help of the neighborhood women was a social event. Medicines were crudely prepared and numerous home cures were developed and used. Many children died during their first few years of life; scarlet fever and diphtheria took the lives of many. In those times, the people didn't have the modern medicines we have today that help protect young children from dreadful diseases and suffering.

Children of colonial times were often named to commemorate a special event or condition at the time they were born. Names such as Easborn or Fathergone were entered in the family Bible. English names were the most popular—George, William, and James were favorites. By the middle of the 1700s, boys were commonly given Biblical names—Peter, Paul, Samuel, and Ezra. Girls were also given English and Biblical names—Elizabeth, Sarah, Abigail, Hannah, Faith, Hope, and Charity.

After a baby was born, it was placed in a cradle that was next to the mother's side of the bed. The parents slept in a high bed, with ropes strung across instead of springs. There was a mattress of corn husks, cotton, or, if the people were very lucky, feathers. Some people had feather coverlets. If there were sheets, they would have been made of linen. All the sheets, blankets, and patchwork quilts were made by the women of the household. The men made the beds and kept the ropes tight. All the material, even the rope, could be produced at home. Only the needles used for the quilting and sewing the hand-woven ticking together to make mattress covers needed to be bought in the general store. Needles and pins were kept in special boxes and taken care of carefully.

There was something called a trundle bed in colonial homes that fit under the parents' bed during the day. This small bed could hold two children. Older children and any

"borning room"

relatives who might have joined the household would probably sleep upstairs where there would be another bedroom. The bathroom was outdoors, in some corner of the woodshed or barn. Later on, there were chamberpots used indoors.

Another piece of colonial furniture was the "settle." This long, wooden bench with a very high straight back was placed in front of the fireplace. The "settle" kept out drafts and also was a cozy place to sit.

Rocking chairs were invented in America during this early period and were commonplace in the colonial home. These early rocking chairs were really just high-backed chairs with "rockers" attached, like the ones on a baby's cradle. The furniture in the colonial home was handmade from wood, simple in design, functional, and extremely durable.

The family usually ate their meals at a long table, which was also used to do their household work on. Meals were soups and spoon-meat—meat made into stews and hash. The people used only a spoon and often held their food in their hands. A wooden noggin or mug held the stew and vegetables, and a pewter tankard held the drink. There were no forks or china to wash. Chairs and benches were used for seats. The colonists also made chests and cabinets for storage. Closets didn't exist in the colonial home.

The floors in the house were usually uncarpeted and some were made of dirt. They had to be swept frequently. If the family was fortunate enough to own a carpet, it would have been hung on the wall or draped over a table, but never put on the floor to be walked on.

The colonial diet was quite varied. The people ate meat, poultry, or seafood twice a day and good amounts of fresh fruits and vegetables in season. Most of the colonists provided all of their own food. The typical family would own a cow, chickens, and ducks, and grow their own fruits, vegetables, and herbs. Neighbors sometimes traded with each other and kept a record of these transactions. They stored the food that they grew themselves or bought at a daily market in storage bins in the cellar. Meat was "cured" with spices and salt, or smoked to preserve it. In the northern colonies, where the winters were cold, some meat could be packed and frozen in the snow. Homemade breads and pies and puddings were enjoyed.

During this entire period, sugar was considered a luxury. Even molasses was costly for the average family. Where sugar maple trees grew, the families could make their own maple syrup. Later on, the colonists had sugaring-off parties. Honey was also scarce during these times. Fortunately, colonial Americans didn't have the same sweet tooth that most of us have today. Instead of the standard sweeteners that we use, they added chopped-up apples, currants, dried blueberries, or pieces of pumpkin or squash to their cake batters. Their cake batter was about as sweet as rich bread dough.

colonial family at dinner

Yeast was the only leavening available. (Yeast is the substance that makes bread and cakes rise.) Baking soda and baking powder weren't introduced until the 1800s. Nutmeg, ginger, and allspice were used in baking, as well as a variety of common herbs, both wild and homegrown. It was not unusual to have an herb garden that was also used for medicinal purposes.

Milk was reserved for the babies of the household. Older children and adults drank apple cider, beer (which was diluted for the children), and tea. Water was thought to be bad for you; it was believed that it sapped your strength.

The colonial kitchen with its large stone fireplace was the center of family life. Parents rose before dawn, poked the hot coals from yesterday's fire, and put the kettle on for tea. The fireplace served as a stove and a source of heat and light for the house. Of course, there wasn't any electricity, so candles were the only other way of lighting the house.

A stock of dry kindling was kept near the hearth to start a fire quickly. Chunks of slow-burning, hard wood would be added next. It took a full hour for the actual fire to die down before a nice bed of red-hot coals was left to cook on. Cooking was done in big kettles and skillets over the open fire. Some of the kettles weighed forty pounds. To broil meats, the colonists had to either hold the meat over the hot coals on the end of a long-handled fork or put it on a spit and turn it three or four times an hour. Corn, potatoes, onions, and nuts were buried in the hot ashes and roasted. Cooking was primitive and time-consuming; it was not until the 1800s that there was a stove that was separate from the fireplace.

America's early homemakers were able to create tasty new ways of preparing the foods that were plentiful in this new land. Many of these wonderful recipes have been handed down through the generations, and with minor changes can still be enjoyed today.

Fashion in early America was set by the styles in Europe and adapted to fit the life styles of the settlers. Styles varied

Stone oven. On the hearth is a bake kettle and a bean pot.

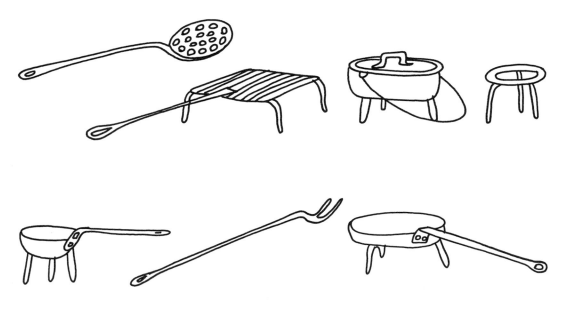

Iron cooking utensils: strainer, gridiron (broiler), bake kettle, trivet (to hold pots), saucepan, toasting fork, spider (frying pan)

from colony to colony. Generally, clothes were simple and constructed for long wear. The sewing was done by hand at home. Each garment required long hours of work. Early Americans had a small wardrobe with only one or two sets of everyday clothes and one Sunday or special outfit.

Everyone in the family was involved with cloth-making. Flax, for fiber, was an important crop on the early American farm. Working raw materials into finished clothing or linen was a long process. The men and boys tended the sheep and the flax crop. The younger children carded and combed the wool or flax fibers into long pieces that were spun into thread or yarn. They gathered berries and bark that were used to make the dyes. The women and girls did the spinning and weaving, although sometimes men were weavers.

The finishing touches of needlework were usually done by the young girls. The sampler was a piece of cloth that was embroidered. It was a kind of practice or learning device for young girls to experiment with. It was also used to learn the alphabet. The most popular stitch used was the cross stitch. Young girls often stitched mottos, friendship vows, or religious sayings as a theme for their samplers. "A stitch in time saves nine" is a common saying. Here is another that was lovingly stitched by a twelve-year-old:

When this you see, remember me,
And keep me in your mind;
And be not like the weather cock
That turn at every wind.

Most samplers were stitched at home, but some were done in school. They were beautifully crafted pieces of needlework that have today become prized pieces of folk art.

As you have seen, the colonial period was an exciting time. The projects that follow will help to bring the colonial home alive. You will be able to share some of the experiences of those days.

Young girls stitching on their samplers

Judith Elaine 1989

Little House Sampler

The embroidered sampler is one of the most charming examples of traditional embroidery. The sampler was first made as a record of stitches, and later as a picture to be framed. The oldest existing sampler dates from the sixteenth century and was made by a little girl named Jane Bostocke in England. The sampler is an embroidered picture of colorful flowers, houses, people, and animals with a verse, usually religious, and an alphabet. Each sampler has the name and age of the person who made it together with the date that she finished her work.

Here's what is needed: ✕✕✕✕✕✕✕✕✕✕✕✕✕✕

12″ square of white or beige linen
tracing paper, carbon paper, pencil, tape
8″ metal or plastic embroidery hoop
embroidery thread in red, yellow, blue, and green
embroidery needle
12″ square of cardboard
14″ square of brightly colored fabric
glue

Here's how to do it:

1. Begin by working on the alphabet part of the sampler. With a pencil, sketch the alphabet on the linen as it is broken up in the design. Center this above the house design, pressing lightly with the pencil.

2. For the rest of the sampler, you will need to trace the designs onto the tracing paper. Then place a piece of carbon paper on the linen. On top of the carbon paper place the tracing paper with the design drawn on it.

3. Carefully tape the three sheets down onto your working surface. This will prevent everything from sliding around.

Draw over the design on the tracing paper with a pencil. Don't press too hard. You will only need a light line to show through on the linen to give you an idea of where to make your stitches.

4. There are illustrations that explain how to do each of the three embroidery stitches used in the making of the sampler. There is also a stitch guide and a color guide.

5. Remove the tracing and carbon papers from the linen. Put some tape along the outside edges of the linen to keep it from fraying.

6. Place the linen in the embroidery hoop and adjust it to fit very tightly. Straighten out the linen so that the surface is smooth and completely free of wrinkles. Now you are ready to stitch.

7. Start with the alphabet. Then complete the house and all the other parts of the design. Checking the illustration for proper placement, lightly write in your name and the date in pencil at the bottom of the sampler. Then stitch over what you have written.

8. To make the frame for your sampler, use the 12″ square of cardboard. Cut an 8″ square from the center of the cardboard to make a "window" to show your sampler. Cover the cardboard frame with the brightly colored fabric by wrapping it around the frame and gluing it to the back. Center the frame over the sampler and tape the sampler in place from the back. Trim it so that it won't go beyond the frame.

Embroidery Stitches

Backstitch

Use the backstitch to embroider the alphabet and your name in. Take one running stitch, then, instead of going forward, for the second and all following stitches, go backward to meet your previous stitch. This will give you a continuous line. Try to make all the stitches the same length. Use this stitch to do the alphabet and the outline of the house. The alphabet should be done in blue and the outline of the house in red.

Cross-Stitch

Make a row of slanting stitches over an equal number of threads of fabric. This forms a row of the first half of each cross. Work back over these stitches as shown. You can also work cross-stitches individually and in any direction, but they must all cross in the same direction. Use this stitch for the borders and to fill inside the house and trees. The borders should be done in red, the house in blue, and the trees in green.

Satin Stitch

This stitch is used where background fabric is to be covered completely. Bring the needle up at one edge of the area to be covered, insert needle at the opposite edge and return to starting line by carrying it underneath the fabric. Try to make the stitches close enough together to cover the background fabric and not too long so that they look loose. You can divide a large area into smaller sections and then work the satin stitch. Use this stitch for the hearts, door, chimneys, windows, and tree trunks. The hearts, door, and chimneys should be done in red. The windows in yellow and the tree trunks in green.

George and Martha

These paper dolls are shown on the opposite page wearing their everyday clothes. Other everyday outfits are shown on pages 27, 28, and 29. Their Sunday best outfits are shown on page 26. Young people wore the same styles, sized to fit them.

George's Sunday best outfit has a wide-brimmed felt hat, waistcoat, fitted vest, and knee breeches. He is wearing a collarless shirt and has a knotted scarf at the neck to finish it off. George is also wearing long wool stockings and leather shoes with shiny buckles.

Martha's finery is a fancy lace cap that she wears to cover her hair, topped with a straw hat. Her long dress has loose-fitting sleeves that are turned back at the elbow. Her chemise, or underdress, extends past the elbows to her wrists. Martha is also wearing a "fichu" or shawl over her shoulders, and black slippers. She also has a basket of flowers and a basket of fruit to carry. Georgina, their pet cat, is wearing a pretty bow.

Here's what is needed:

oaktag (for the paper dolls)
tracing paper, carbon paper, white paper (for their clothes)
scissors, pencil, tape
colored felt-tip markers, black fine-line felt-tip marker

Here's how to do it:

1. Place a sheet of tracing paper over George and Martha and their clothes and trace them.

2. Place a sheet of carbon paper over the oaktag that you will be using to make the people and on the white paper for their clothes. On top of the carbon paper place the tracing paper with the design on it.

3. Gently tape the three sheets together at the top and bottom onto your working surface. This will prevent the papers from sliding around as you draw. Draw over the design on the tracing paper.

4. Remove the tracing and carbon papers. With the black fine-line felt-tip marker, draw over the designs. Cut them out. Color with the other markers.

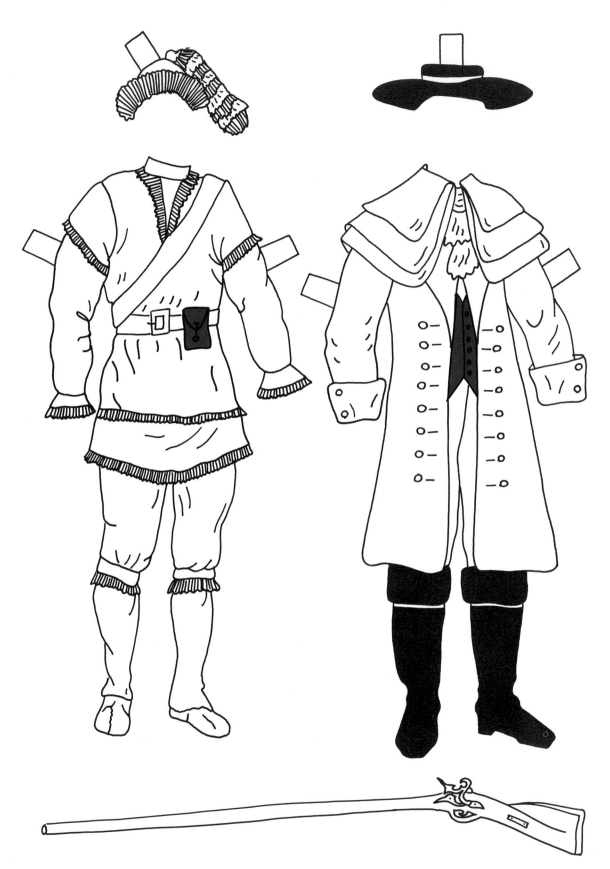

Holly

Abigail

Elizabeth

Amy

Jennifer

Sandra

Ruth

Friends' Friendship Pillow

Colonial women worked on "friendship quilts" together with relatives and friends. Each lady wrote her name in a corner of the quilt block that she made. When all the quilt squares were completed, they were sewn together and then quilted together to form a warm and comfy quilt for a loved one. All the quilt blocks together, each one signed by the quilter, reminded the quilt's owner of all the friends who had gathered together to make a special gift. You can remember your friends with this special little friendship pillow.

Here's what is needed:

two pieces of 10″ square muslin, pencil, scissors
black permanent felt-tip marker, colored embroidery floss
straight pins, needle, thread, cotton balls

Here's how to do it:

1. Have your friends sign their names on both muslin squares with the felt-tip marker. Be careful to write at least one inch away from the outside edges of the muslin. You can also decorate your pillow with some pretty embroidered flowers. Check the illustration for ideas.

2. With a pencil, lightly draw the flowers wherever you want them. Embroider over the pencil lines using the backstitch. (See page 23.)

3. After you have finished decorating both sides of the pillow, pin the two pieces of muslin together with the right sides facing each other. Sew all around the outside edge leaving a 4″ opening. Turn the pillow right side out and stuff it with the cotton balls. Sew up the opening.

dower chest

Colonial Chests

When the settlers came to America, they brought with them cherished souvenirs of the Old World in chests. Chests were some of the earliest pieces of furniture and were even made in ancient Egypt. They first were used to lock away church treasures. Later on, during the Middle Ages, each home had several chests in which the family heirlooms were kept.

Eventually, special chests were made for a young girl to fill with treasures for her wedding. Bridal or dower chests became important to every young woman. By the time a colonial girl was eight or nine, she probably had a bridal or dower chest of her own. Besides her household and personal items, the girl stored her needlework there, knowing that one day it would decorate her home.

Colonial furniture makers carried on the tradition of making these wonderful chests and did some of their finest work producing them. These chests were valued as works of art as well as for the riches that they held.

The most popular dower chests came from Pennsylvania German furniture makers. These often were painted in soft greens and blues. Against this background, fanciful motifs were applied, many of them reminiscent of the Old-World tradition of manuscript illustration.

Typically, the front of the Pennsylvania German chests had three decorated panels. The two outside panels were given matching designs; the painter added his name or the initials of the owner and the date the chest was made to the design on the center panel.

Besides these chests, deed and document boxes were made and used in colonial America. They were also hand-painted, decorated with designs made with sponges or combs, or with simple bands of color. Now you can make and enjoy one of the boxes and use it to store your treasures.

Colonial Chest Treasure Box

This makes a perfect hideaway for personal treasures and is very pretty with the early American designs on it. Designs are given for flowers, hearts, and a small house surrounded by trees. The leaves of the trees are made by using a sponge dipped in paint. This is the way they were actually done and it is great fun!

Here's what is needed:

a sturdy box with a top (a candy box or shoe box works well)
black felt-tip marker
poster paints—tan, light green, dark green, dark red,
and dark brown
paintbrush, clean jar with water in it (to wash brushes in)
1″ piece of sponge, aluminum foil

Here's how to do it:

1. First paint the entire box with the tan poster paint. Allow it to dry for about an hour.

2. With the black felt-tip marker, draw the house, hearts, and flowers onto the box. Check the illustration.

3. With the brush, paint the tree trunks using the dark brown paint. Check the illustration.

4. Put a small amount of dark green paint on the aluminum foil and dip the sponge into it. Checking the illustration, gently stamp the sponge onto the trees to form leaves.

5. You can use this same method to make grass along the bottom of the box using the light green paint. Also check the illustration for ideas.

Bountiful Bread

Here's a schedule that many colonial families liked to follow: Sunday was a go-to-meeting day, Monday was washday, Tuesday was ironing day, Wednesday was mending day, Thursday was get-together day, Friday was cleaning day, and Saturday was baking day.

Saturday was when a week's supply of bread was made by the women of the house. Bread, rolls, several pies, cakes, doughnuts, and cookies were all baked and enjoyed by the whole family.

The smell of freshly baked bread is one of the most welcome aromas to come out of a kitchen. A thick slice of bread warm from the oven, topped with a melting slab of butter, is certainly one of the most delicious foods of all time.

In colonial times, farms grew grains—wheat, oats, barley, and rye. Most of these grains were used to feed the animals, and the rest was used for the family. Grain was ground into flour for home use at the village mill.

Ingredients:

¾ cup lukewarm water
2 packages active dry yeast
1¼ cups milk
4½ to 5 cups flour
¼ cup butter, softened
2 tablespoons sugar
2 teaspoons baking powder
1 teaspoon salt
extra flour to roll out the dough
extra butter, softened, to
    grease the loaf pan and to
    spread on the bread (about
    4 tablespoons)

Utensils:

large mixing bowl
mixing spoon
measuring cups and spoons
rolling pin
9″ × 5″ × 3″ metal loaf pan
clean dish cloth

Here's how to do it:

1. Grease the loaf pan with some of the extra butter.

2. Put the lukewarm water into the large bowl and then stir in the yeast. Add the milk, 2½ cups flour, the ¼ cup butter, sugar, baking powder, and salt. Beat until completely combined.

3. Now stir in the remaining flour to give a soft and slightly sticky dough. Knead the dough on a floured surface until it is smooth and not sticky anymore. You do this by pressing the dough with the palms of your hands, adding a little flour, until the dough stretches easily. This should take from three to five minutes.

4. With the rolling pin, roll the dough into an 18″ by 9″ rectangle. With your hands, roll up the short side of the dough and press the ends to seal it closed. Place the loaf with the seam side down in the loaf pan.

5. With more of the extra butter, coat the top of the bread. Cover the bread with the clean dish cloth and let it rise in a warm place where there are no drafts. The bread will double in size. It should rise at least two inches above the pan in the center. This takes about an hour. Preheat the oven to 425°; ask an adult to help you with this. Bake the bread for 30–35 minutes or until the loaf is golden. Enjoy!

Shrewsbury Cakes

These delicious sugar cookies, or Shrewsbury cakes as they were called in colonial days, originated in England. They can be made either flat or rolled out and cut into little heart shapes. Share them with your friends.

Ingredients:

¾ cup butter, softened
1¼ cups sugar
1 egg
1½ teaspoons grated orange peel
2 teaspoons vanilla
2½ cups sifted all-purpose flour
½ teaspoon salt
extra sugar

Utensils:

large mixing bowl
mixing spoon
measuring cups and spoons
waxed paper
small glass
pencil, cardboard, scissors
knife, spatula
cookie sheets, wire racks

Here's how to do it:

1. Cream—beat—the butter and sugar together. Add the egg, grated orange peel, and the vanilla.

2. Stir in the flour and salt to make a stiff dough. Wrap the dough in waxed paper. Refrigerate for several hours or overnight.

3. Roll the dough into 1-inch balls and then roll the balls in sugar. Arrange the balls 1½ inches apart on ungreased cookie sheets. Flatten the balls gently with the bottom of a small glass.

4. Preheat the oven to 350°; ask an adult to help you with this. Put the cookie sheets into the oven and bake for about 8 minutes or until the cookies are lightly browned on the edges.

5. Remove the cookies from the oven and with a spatula put them on wire racks to cool. Makes about 3 dozen cookies.

Note: You could also make heart-shaped cookies. To use the heart-shaped cookie pattern, draw the pattern on clean cardboard and cut it out. Roll the dough to a ¼ inch thickness on a lightly floured surface. Lay the pattern on the rolled-out dough and cut around the pattern with a knife. With the spatula, place the cookies on the cookie sheets about an inch apart. Sprinkle the cookies with the extra sugar before baking.

Stirabout

This is a thick chicken stew that was served in colonial homes and taverns. It was cooked in one pot.

Ingredients:

4 cups chicken broth
4 cups sliced potatoes
1 cup chopped celery
1 teaspoon parsley
1 teaspoon garlic powder
1 teaspoon salt
1 teaspoon white pepper
2 cups cooked chicken, cut
   into small pieces
2 cups canned corn (drained)
1 cup tomato sauce
2 eggs, beaten
½ cup all-purpose flour

Utensils:

large saucepan with cover
mixing spoon
small mixing bowl
fork and teaspoon

Here's how to do it:

1. Bring the chicken broth to a boil in a large saucepan.

2. Add the potatoes, celery, parsley, garlic powder, salt, and pepper. Simmer, covered, until the potatoes are almost tender, 15 to 20 minutes.

3. Add the cooked chicken, tomato sauce, and canned corn.

4. In a small bowl, beat the eggs and flour with a fork to make a thin paste. Drop by teaspoonfuls into the boiling broth. Cover and gently boil for about 8 to 10 minutes. Makes six servings.

Journey Cake

There are many varieties of this biscuit-like cake, originally called a "Shawnee Cake" because it came from an Indian recipe. Then it was called a "Journey Cake," since it stayed fresh for several days and could be taken along by travelers.

Ingredients:

1 cup cornmeal
1 cup flour
½ teaspoon salt
½ teaspoon baking soda
2 eggs, beaten
2 cups milk
2 tablespoons molasses
vegetable oil to grease the
    baking dish

Utensils:

large mixing bowl
measuring cups and spoons
mixing spoon
8″ baking dish

Here's how to do it:

1. Preheat the oven to 350°; ask an adult to help you with this.

2. Mix together the cornmeal, flour, salt, and baking soda.

3. Add the eggs, milk, and molasses, stirring until completely combined.

4. Grease the baking pan.

5. Pour the batter into the baking pan and place in the oven. Bake for about 20 minutes.

Queen's Cake

This very old recipe makes a special cake "fit for a queen." It uses the finest and most costly ingredients of the day. Since cookbooks didn't exist in colonial America until around the 1740s and they were still scarce then, women usually exchanged recipes of their own. They carefully wrote down favorite recipes in a handmade book or on a sheet of paper. Early cooks had an abundance of good food available to them and served many wonderful meals. This cake might have been made at home or at a bake shop in town.

Ingredients:

1½ cups raisins
1 cup butter, softened
1 cup sugar
5 eggs, beaten
1 teaspoon orange extract
2 teaspoons lemon extract
2 cups sifted all-purpose
  flour
½ teaspoon baking powder
½ teaspoon cinnamon
extra butter to grease the
  baking pan
1 extra tablespoon of flour to
  coat the raisins

Utensils:

large mixing bowl
mixing spoon
measuring cups and spoons
waxed paper
9″ × 5″ × 3″ loaf pan
toothpick

Here's how to do it:

1. Grease the loaf pan with the extra butter.

2. Preheat the oven to 350°; ask an adult to help you with this.

3. Spread out the raisins on a sheet of waxed paper and then coat them with the tablespoon of flour.

4. Combine the butter and sugar in the large mixing bowl. Stir them together until they are creamy.

5. Add the eggs and orange and lemon extracts. Now add the flour, baking powder, and cinnamon.

6. Put the raisins into the batter and stir until they are combined. Pour the batter into the loaf pan and bake for 1 hour and 20 minutes or until a toothpick inserted into the center of the cake comes out clean. Allow cake to cool and then remove from pan and slice.

Christmas Fruit Cake

This moist and delicious Christmas fruit cake is a very colorful one because of the bits of chopped candied cherry, candied pineapple, candied orange peel, and raisins that are in it. The recipe for the candied orange peel is in the *Village* book on page 46.

Ingredients:

1 cup butter, softened
6 eggs
3 cups all-purpose flour
½ teaspoon salt
¼ teaspoon baking soda
2¾ cups sugar
1 teaspoon lemon extract
½ teaspoon vanilla
1 cup dairy sour cream
1 cup of chopped candied
    cherries, candied pineap-
    ple, and candied orange
    peel (total of 1 cup)
½ cup golden raisins
extra butter to grease the
    pan
confectioners' sugar, sifted

Utensils:

large mixing bowl
mixing spoon
measuring cups and spoons
10″ tube pan
toothpick

Here's how to do it:

1. Preheat the oven to 350°; ask an adult to help you with this.

2. Grease the tube pan with the extra butter.

3. In the large mixing bowl, combine the butter and the eggs. Beat until fluffy. Add the flour, salt, and baking soda.

44

4. Add the sugar, scraping the bowl frequently. Continue to mix the batter until it is completely combined.

5. Add the lemon extract and vanilla. Now add the sour cream and stir until the batter is creamy.

6. Finally, add the colorful bits of chopped fruit, which all together totals one cup. Add the raisins, and stir until everything is combined.

7. Put the batter into the greased tube pan. Bake in the oven for about 1½ hours or until done. A toothpick inserted into the cake should come out clean and the top of the cake should have a golden color. Allow the cake to cool, and then sift some confectioners' sugar over the cake. Makes about 16 servings.

Blueberry Jam

Farm-fresh produce and rich dairy products were abundant ingredients in colonial cooking. Freshly picked strawberries and blueberries were a special treat. A sunny afternoon spent berry picking was a young person's delight.

Ingredients for Blueberry Jam:

4 medium-sized apples, peeled, cored, and finely chopped
2 cups water
4 cups fresh blueberries (or frozen)
3¾ cups sugar

Utensils:

large saucepan
mixing spoon, fork
6 clean half-pint jars with covers

Here's how to do it:

1. Mix the apples and water in a large saucepan. Simmer until the apples are soft, 15 to 20 minutes. If necessary, mash the apples with a fork.

2. Add the berries; simmer another 5 minutes.

3. Add the sugar; bring the mixture to a boil. Continue to boil for 5 to 6 minutes.

4. Pour mixture into jars. This jam lasts for several months when stored in the refrigerator. It is delicious on homemade bread or ice cream and makes a welcome gift.

Strawberry Jam

This delicious jam is quick to make and wonderful on freshly baked bread.

Ingredients for Strawberry Jam: **Utensils:**

4 cups strawberries, washed and with the stems cut off
3 cups sugar

large saucepan
measuring cups
mixing spoon
4 twelve-ounce glass jars with lids

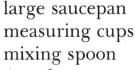

Here's how to do it:

1. In a large saucepan, crush the strawberries and add the sugar. Let the mixture stand until the sugar is dissolved, about 15 minutes.

2. Now put the saucepan on the stove and bring the mixture to a boil. Turn down the heat and continue to cook for about 3 more minutes.

3. Remove the saucepan from the heat. After the mixture has cooled, spoon it into clean glass jars that have tight-fitting lids. Store in the refrigerator. Makes 4 twelve-ounce jars of jam.

Index

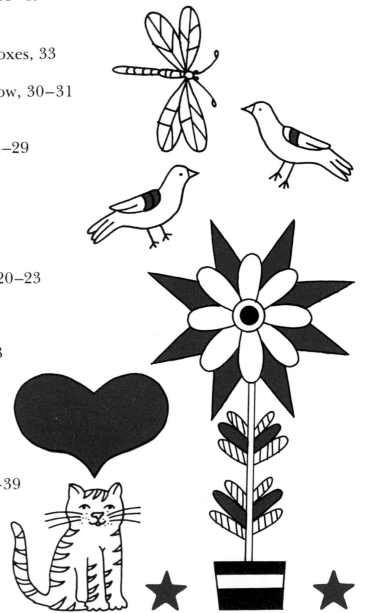